FIRST PERSON PLURAL

poems

by

R. N. TABER

"Colour, creed, sex, sexuality…these are but part of a whole.
It is the whole that counts."

First published in Great Britain in 2002 by Assembly Books,
C-Hammond House, 45a Gaisford Street, London NW5 2EB

Copyright 2002

ISBN 0-9539833-1-5

Typesetting, layout and cover design: ProPrint, Riverside
Cottages, Old Great North Road, Stibbington, Cambs. PE8
6LR

Also by R. N. Taber: *Love And Human Remains: poems*
Assembly Books, ©2000
ISBN 0-9539833-0-7

DEDICATION

SEE-HEAR

A blur of silence all around
closing in on me...
all I sought yet never found

A yearning for the sound
of bird and bee...
a blur of silence all around

Oh, to leap life's merry-go-round,
for a chance to be...
all I sought yet never found

Then you ran me to ground
persistently...
a blur of silence all around

I heard the sweetest sound
within me...
all I sought yet never found.

Such songs this heart confound
you taught me...
A blur of silence all around,
all I sought yet never found

<u>Note</u>: As a partially deaf person, I know only too well some of the problems facing those with any degree of hearing loss. It is, however, only as big a problem as we choose to make it and most of us choose not to let it interfere with the way we live our lives.

Certainly, it is less of a 'disability' than the attitude of many hearing people towards us. A gay poet, therefore, frequently faces something of a double-whammy since the attitude of many heterosexual people towards gays also leaves much to be desired. Thankfully, attitudes - in both respects - continue to change and, on the whole, for the better.

CONTENTS:

PART I: ASPECTS OF ECOLOGY

AMERICAN POEMS (1999):

PART II: FIRST PERSON PLURAL

PART III: GAY'S THE WORD

PART V: LOST AND FOUND

[i]First published in an anthology of the same name by Poetry Now, 2001; subsequently awarded a 2nd prize in the Forward Press annual competition and appeared in its *Top 100 Poets, 2001*. (The poem, *Ordinary People - see* my first major collection, *Love And Human Remains* - also won a 2nd prize and appeared in *Top 100 Poets,* 1999).

[ii]Dedication: David is an American friend who lives in San Francisco, Ca.

[iii]Dedication: Steven and Tina are American friends who live in Sacramento, Ca. with their son Zachary.

[iv]Dedication: Richard is an artist and teacher friend who lives in London.

[v]Dedication: Shaun is one of many new friends I have made since going online in 1998.

[vi]Dedication: Liz is a writer based in London. We met on a school trip to Paris in the 1960s, lost touch during the 1970s and met up again by chance in 2000.

[vii]Originally written as a song lyric; first published in a poetry anthology, 2001.

[viii]A slightly different version of this poem first appeared under the title *On Bereavement* in *How Can You Write A Poem When You're Dying Of Aids* - edited by John Harold - Cassell, 1993; a second edited version appeared as *World Without End* in *The Path of Destiny*, Poetry Now 2002.

[ix]Dedication: Don was married with grown-up children when he finally came to terms with his sexuality. Sadly, many people still cannot find it in their hearts to support such a brave step.

[x]A different version of this poem appeared under the title *Pink Gin* in *August And Genet,* Aramby Publications, 1996.

[xi]This poem first appeared in *A Time Of Trial,* Hidden Brook Press (Canada) 200l, compiled within a few months of the September 11th tragedies in the U.S.A. I have since revised the last few stanzas.

PART ONE

ASPECTS OF ECOLOGY

A WINTER'S TALE

A massive spearhead of shadow
invades the glorious sunset
(once victorious sunset!)
pierces each violet vein of light
till bloody streamers
blot the moon

Weasel lurks at the edge of moody ice,
phantom of this half world

Watch the sun dying,
my dying son,
see the spidery moonlight spread
like tardy concerns on Judgement Day
as ghosts of our recent dead
come out to play

ASPECTS OF ECOLOGY

Flowers in the garden
looking pretty;
Bees making honey
at the hive;
Kids in class, learning
about life

Daisies on the lawn
mowed down;
Queen bee robbed
blind;
Out of sight, out
of mind

WILDLIFE ON ONE

Badger blinks an eye
at dimming stars;
Owl scoops up a mole
and heads for base;
Leaves rustle cautiously
around the nest;
Rabbits dart here
and there, like
exocets

Owl's gliding low;
Badger stays put;
Sounds of morning
have no greeting
but hover like a lark
struck dumb - by
the fingers at its neck
of a plague wind
from Iraq

A TOUCH OF FROST

Snow leopard defending
its territory;
Eagle circling
its prey;
Wolf howling to others
across eternity;
Avalanche stirring...
even as we wait
for winter's cruelty
to abate;
Tears on pillows, shapes
on frosty windows;
Scraps of tinsel, leftover
Christmas;
Too cold for snow,
too late for us?

Watery sun, marking
the beasts of spring

SNAKES ALIVE

Creeps across the world
like a pretty snake,
insinuating each word,
every move we make

Does not discriminate,
nor its slow poison
a ready antidote
for anyone

Treading with careless step,
each to our own Eden,
risks a beauty skin deep
getting even

A snake in the grass
called Loneliness

KILLING FIELDS

Life, death, hawk's wings between
rainbow hues; chirruping among yews
in a country churchyard;
Cock's making a clamour, fox
sneaking the coop, all Nature
running heaven's loop;
Life, death, a seabird's flair
for diving swell (albatross, alive
and well at the helm);
Whales hunted down by global
powers, defying heaven's
own watchtowers;
Life, death, hawk's on the lookout;
Fox hears a shout; cock's reprieved;
At sea, sanity of sorts;
In a hurricane's eye,
dare Man and Nature finally
call a truce?

Bold new century, old gods
laughing at us

HIROSHIMA MON AMOUR

Falling, falling

Singed leaves
to the grief-hung
ground gravely
given

Falling, falling

Skylarks
where we played
till noon-dark
forbade

Calling, calling

Politicians
at their damnedest
to do themselves
proud

Weeping cloud

REQUIEM FOR A SKYLARK

On tuneful wing, our seasons
scanning, circles and dips
anxiously a covenant
with Earth's poetry, where
once a nesting tree
grew tall

Now, a shopping
mall

NATURE TRAIL

Follow leafy trails
into red and orange,
silver, green;
Let the dew of life
wash clean our
dirty hands;
Be still, antic winds
till nothing's heard
but an egg-bird;
A tear in the eye;
All our yesterdays
on standby

OUTLOOK, CHANGEABLE

Smoky old town,
draped in oily twilight
during a winter rain;
Among glistening spires,
a tolling bell conspires
to wake the dead;
Memories blur - in each
boiled head, running
for cover;
A heavy air, dragging
on the feet - like
naked fear;
Kisses, like market wine;
Poison darts - in the
bloodstream;
Storm, all but passed;
Nature, on cue
for a revival

World, counting the cost
of our survival

RIDDLE OF THE SANDS

Crossing a desert,
hump on the back, sniffing
for oasis and shade,
penetrating mirage on mirage,
desecrating hopeful visage
with pricks of sand, graffiti
on the soul, moving finger
of a rag doll

Crossing a desert,
hump on the back, sniffing
for oasis and shade,
under the spell of an adventure
culture, drawn into Dante's
inferno, no matter vultures
circling like dealers
at a disco

Crossing a desert,
hump on the back, sniffing
for oasis and shade,
compensating delusion with
illusion, blisters on the soul
down to Lords of Misrule
though (trick or treat)
it's our call

East west, north, south,
which way, truth?

A GARDENER'S WORLD

Ageing heart, a quiet garden,
its blooms a pride and joy
walled in for protection
against heavy tread
of girl or boy

Ageing heart, seeks privacy,
rejects intimacy, prefers
the company of ghosts
than concede
temporality

Ageing heart, a lonely soul,
heard laughter one day,
broke down the wall,
let children in
to play

Ageing heart, a prize garden
in high-rise flat or country cot;
among all its flowers,
an old favourite,
forget-me-not

TRASHING THE MILLENNIUM

Oceans, a dumping ground
for Man's trash;
Concerns that sea life may perish
turning on the prosperity
of our fishermen – and a yearning
for cod on the plate;
Galaxy, a dumping ground
for Man's ambition;
Life forms, even human,
fair game - but lesser clones
spinning away out of sight
so no real harm done
in the name of Progress
that future generations
might yet accuse us
of sinning our way
to godliness?

VIEW FROM A TIME MACHINE

Leaves in a ditch, drifting
like tears in the wind;
A frantic scratching at the earth
while there's still time
before eternal frost – and
all seems lost, once won
under the sun;
Desolation, the eye seeks
and cannot see;
Isolation, the heart longs
a thriving peace,
better seasons, reasons for all
that's lost, once won
under the sun;
In uncut grass, long shadows
dancing on the graves of loved ones
left for "Missing, believed Dead"
under wet pillows;
O, cruel world, our freedom thrall
to all that's left unsaid, undone
under the sun

Twilight zone

PREMATURE EJACULATION

Tread softly, angel
on my dreams;
Heaven is not
the place it seems;
Out of dawn's early rain
into high noon
let's press on
though twilight
come

Again, too soon

TOWARDS A COMING OF AGE

Darling buds of spring
remain closed in the branches
of a tree, once climbed
by the child I was

Your letters, unopened
in a drawer

TRACKS

On a blade of grass,
a snail leaves its mark;
In Brussels, politicians
discuss pensions;
On a tree trunk,
lovers pledge themselves;
In Washington, Congress
debating landmines;
In bus shelters, street kids
sign graffiti;
At world conferences,
token gestures

AUTUMN LEAVES

Pavement art
at heaven's door
left ajar

A love affair, one
summer

A HORSEMAN RIDING BY

Out of the corner
of an eye,
we saw a horseman
passing by,
casting long shadows,
pricking the nerves,
fair cutting a dash
in a cocked hat;
Bold mare, playing
her part;
Spurs, egging on
smoky flesh
like fingernails at
our shoulders;
Free rein, riding
under fire...
into songs, stories,
hearts' desire

Clouds passing,
birds cheering

GLOBAL WARNING

O world, of love and beauty!
Nature's glory all around;
Sad, a devil's cruelty
in Man's own story found

O world, such creatures in it
of every shape and colour!
Man, selling off the planet
for an easy dollar

O world, an Eden bound to lose!
History, repeating our mistakes;
Lion kings born in eco-zoos;
Mercenaries raising the stakes

O world, defying an ozone crack;
Beware! Nature's fighting back

A HYMN TO SPRING

Spring is here at last,
wintry days passed;
In the air, birds singing;
Everywhere, bluebells
ringing out a message
of peace and love - through
a passage of seasons,
short cut to Eternity, where
the heart has its reasons
for secrecy and the soul
intones rites in the wind,
that secure a future
for mankind ;
Summer, autumn, winter…
Life, but a passing shadow
come and gone;
No mere chance thing,
but a never-ending story
as told in the *Gloria*
of spring

AMNESTY

Feathers of sound, winging
a merry breeze...
bringing life's music
to deaf shores;
Breeze pauses mischievously
to jig on slump shoulders;
Feathers hover, around
a heavy knee;
Heart protests. Feathers fly.
Soul, veering on abyss,
saved by a pie-bird's
return kiss;
Last seen winging nursery
rhyme on factory walls,
graffiti for a late
wake-up call;
Up and away, courtesy
of heaven's unlikely
amnesty for all
prisoners

JACOB'S LADDER

See
the poplar
sway, envy grace
a nesting place,
clamber clouds,
meet God head-on;
Transparent, this day!
All its worth clear to me,
all on earth dear to me
and all I cannot be
sticks in my
throat

LIGHTNING

I strike without warning
and drums applaud;
Injury or death – who
falls on my sword;
Even trees of the forest fear
when I am near – and
birds keep to the nest
that know best;
Petals close – and heaven
looks on as I choose to chide
humanity's darker side
for its complacency
in matters of Peace;
Nor shall I ever cease
to show animal, vegetable,
friend or foe, though Man
may rule the Earth – by politics
or religion, blaming mistakes
on a God in heaven;
I wait in the wings, quick
and powerful, to fly in the face
of things temporal, following
no godly course, this angry
angel turned loose
on the world

Bringing word

SPOILS OF WAR

Shadows gathering like crowds
for an execution;
Storm clouds rumbling, like
a malediction on
the planet;
Time to bow out, right here
and now? In a spotlight
of sunshine, luminous
corn circles tracing
the mystery - of
our history;
Parts played out.
Hearts on a rout - beaten
by a native savagery
plaguing the beauty
of our humanity

To Nature, its dignity - or
Progress, a poor victory

STORM WARNING

We watched elephants
rumbling across the sky,
feet crashing, trumpets blowing,
terror in each eye, herded
into chaos by real estate
bosses, sights set on
the tourist industry,
holiday homes,
package safari

We ran through the rain,
found squatters at home,
tried breaking in, police moved
us on, nothing to be done;
For now, at least, making
the best of a bad situation,
makeshift accommodation
while the law runs
its course

Poetic justice?

DRIVING CONDITIONS

New year stretching ahead
like the M1 in early hours?
A riot of emotion in the head
turning upon last year's below par
performance; a yearning come
to nothing? No harm in dreams
so long as they don't take over
and reality becomes nothing more
than cover for a lonely heart;
Get real. (Stay wide-awake
at the wheel, for a start);
Heading for Tinsel Town?
Don't let Santa get you down
because he missed you out;
It's your shout. Stop the car.
Look around. Beauty everywhere.
Let the heart feast, the soul gladdened
to a fullness of Being than saddened
by a worldliness found wanting.
Coast along. Sing a proud song
loud enough for the world to hear
and share a Happy New Year

Travel safely, arrive hopefully

CLOUDS ACROSS THE SUN

Shacks, tumbling each other;
Children, chasing shadows
while twilight lasts;
A shy youth looks on sullenly
at giggling virgins
by a well;
Macho towers, vying with
palm trees for more
shoulder room;
Here, a ritual mourning;
There, a routine birth;
War's the shout;
Someone, close to starving;
Someone, making
a profit;
Blind Hannah, observing
AIDS - taken paradise
by surprise;
Sun gods, on a package
tour - around
an oyster

See Africa

THE WORLD THIS WEEKEND

In pastures green, desert sand
slither silent, unseen,
lessons unlearned

Fear - like a dead man's hand
appears sound, washed clean
in pastures green, desert sand

Words - like swords at the land
ripping out its spleen,
lessons unlearned

Love - a living, moving strand
of hope on the world scene
in pastures green, desert sand

Time - to make a stand,
against war and pain,
lessons unlearned?

Faith - keep us safe and sound
nor leave our wounds unclean
in pastures green, desert sand,
lessons unlearned

'AMERICAN' POEMS

This selection comprises poems written during my first visit to the United States in September/October 1999. I spent some time in California before travelling on the Amtrak trains from San Francisco to Boston. Finally, I stayed a few days in New York and flew home. Although travelling on my own, I can honestly say I was never lonely. I saw beautiful scenery, visited fascinating places, met a variety of wonderful people and made some good friends. Instead of taking photographs, I sketched first impressions and feelings in the form of draft poems and worked on them later.

Some of the time, I travelled in the footsteps of Arthur Atkins (1873-1899) - a young artist and occasional poet who migrated to the San Francisco Bay area from Liverpool in the 1890s. I did some research on Atkins for an artist friend, Steven Muzylowski, who lives in Sacramento and this inspired my trip. (See my "Dedication" poem and Note in *Love And Human Remains*).

The 'California' poems were later published in the *Central California Poetry Journal*, 2001 and remain on its web site. *New York, New York* first appeared in a U.K. (Poetry Today) anthology, 2001.

GOLDEN GATE
(For David)

O, wide and tawny land!
Coastal range that rolls but gently
as if to assuage the greater fears
of those who come as strangers
seeking a wealth even above gold
within a tangled web of tales told
of those who came before - pioneers
brave and steadfast in spite of more
(far more) than human spirit
should endure

O, wide and tawny land!
Harboring bear in a City of Dreams,
where fog rolls like the mountains,
obscuring satisfaction with all that needs
be done - to draw a restless spirit home.
No distraction. Closeted in personal space,
rediscovering a precious identity.
Passing on. Come the sun, choices
clearing, a wealth of nations
all-enduring

FEEDING THE DRAGON

Good times clinging to the rail
heading for the skies, like
a dragon's tail;
Sun on the face, a joy to share
with nations of the world
in a cable car;
Laughter has a language
of its own - second
to none;
A sense of integration,
only halfway
to heaven;
Suddenly, journey ends,
world rushes in through
a camera lens,
marking out the same
old boundaries
again;
Scales of a dragon
misting over
the sun

DAYS OF BEAR AND ROSES

California sunshine opens up
my heart, like petals
of a summer rose;
A poem grows, proud and free
like Bear all around
on the streets, in hills
that surround;
Though in a misty rainfall,
each word disappears,
its presence a comfort still
on California ears,
like the songs of pioneers
that inspire us all
to plant poems, in
our home soil;
Through sunshine and rain,
our seasons turn again, again;
Yet, may summer roses
help ease our pain...
and poems, proud and free
about Bear - in
gold country

SACRAMENTO HOME
(For Steven & Tina)

Walking in the old town,
soaking up the poetry;
Waiting at the station,
journey into history;
Chatting with pioneers
past-into-future;
Town, built on more than
bricks and mortar;
Oh, spirit of a country!
Glorious endeavour;
Street festivals, a victorious
pulling together;
Men and women of courage
on the Capitol walls;
California heritage, in
sidewalk footfalls;
Ordinary people, carrying
within each striving soul
seeds of hope and love
and freedom's call;
An ear for the music of life
wherever we roam;
No finer rhythm than
Sacramento home

*As the river flows, so
our story goes*

A MODERN GOTHIC

Ferry to Salem, spray in the hair
like the tongues of witches at each ear,
weaving spells to magic us where
once a child would look;
House of Seven Gables
in a storybook;
Arrive, start queuing for a guide,
though only the witches will understand
how some know this House better
than life-lines inscribed
like runes on each
trembling hand;
A writing desk; ghosts gathering
for the daily seduction of those tourists
risen above a potted history
of literary legacy, searching the mirror
every day - for a scarlet
letter 'A';
Later, let the mid-day sun
seduce Imagination with poems
by Whitman, legends of Walden,
tales of Huck Finn...
and one, Nathaniel Hawthorne's
wicked perception;
Witches, casting spells;
Writers, telling tales; the rest of us
abandoning Seven Gables - for other
ponderables, lurching from
one century to another, stirring
home brews

NEW YORK, NEW YORK

Civilization, on a roll

Tamed land, testing its soul on
Wall Street. Nine-to-fivers in a rush
to beat fellow survivors to the Internet,
earn the right to take a shower,
put up their feet, do the town
(on credit). On the sidewalk,
a steel band, marketing
the Promised Land

Civilization, on a roll

Central Park, good for a stroll
when the heat's on; oases of quiet water
like cameos of family life sparkling
in the sun. St Thomas's, but a stone's
throw away on the Avenue open
all hours - a Gothic charm among
Fortune's towers, to office hours
no thrall

Civilization, on a roll

PART TWO

FIRST PERSON PLURAL

THE POET'S SONG

I am a Painter of Dreams,
my brush, a pen – words
all the paint available, tackling
the unassailable to bring within reach
of unquiet heart, restless soul,
images of life and love,
vision of a goal beyond perimeters
of time, space - humanity's crude
conception of grace

I am a Painter of Dreams,
bringing you mine, intruding
on yours, winging heaven's
elusive towers that flicker in a mist
of aspiration, inviting inspiration,
daring us to home in, defy
the rude mentality of a classroom
morality - humanity's crude
conception of spirituality

Look, see hear, taste, touch, smell.
I am a Painter of Dreams, who
means well but often offends
who dare suggest I speak for all
that seek gold where the rainbow ends;
For, like Pandora's Box, our secrets
once let fly - each to their own;
Painter, dreamer, shades of light
or ships in a cruel night

Senses, falling apart at the seams
for a Painter of Dreams

ODE TO LOVE

Walking the world with you,
smiles for everyone...
under a patch of blue

Making time for a view
or just having fun...
walking the world with you

Sometimes rain, it's true
and we have to run...
under a patch of blue

Stars fall, wishes come true,
one by one...
walking the world with you

Nor shall death win through,
twin souls undone...
under a patch of blue

May heaven guide true
for everyone...
walking the world with you
under a patch of blue

MEN AND WOMEN
(For Richard)

Man or woman…
if you love them
it's everything
and you'll hear birds sing
in Camden market
if you get it right;
Get it wrong and hear
a different song
all our days,
spent wandering a maze
of wishful thoughts
on lonely streets,
always grumbling about
pigeon droppings
and dog mess,
cyclists in shopping malls
and drivers making
mobile calls,
jealous of other people's
seeming capacity
for happiness,
gleaning comfort
as and when
we can

Man or woman

FIRST PERSON PLURAL

I'd amble quiet shores
so waves could thrill me
with tales of heroes,
ride a fluffy cloud,
no matter gulls mocking
my every mood,
often catch a glimpse,
resent your presence;
You, a mere intrusion
into bitter-sweet illusion;
Then I barely saw you
for a while, nor cloud,
wave or gull...
till I heard a shout
as you found me
out

ALL FINGERS AND THUMBS

Sun on the face brought
tears to my eyes;
Saw your mouth move, watched
decision in your look...
crush blades of spring grass
between finger and thumb

A long, hot summer pursued
my confusion;
Panting at the breast, eager for
sandy promises - till you went
and smashed the hourglass
between finger and thumb

Rain on the face hid
tears in my eyes;
Saw your mouth move, watched
decision in your look...
crush us, like autumn leaves
between finger and thumb

MOTHER LOVE

I hear an angel crying
for the joy of a child newly born;
a lovely, gentle human being
to live and love, laugh and mourn
through tears of its own;
I hear an angel singing
for the joy of a child newly grown;
a lovely, gentle human being
risen above worldly troubles
down to human foibles;
I see an angel winging
for the joy of someone's passing;
a lovely, gentle human being
taken at last, deserving of rest
among the best;
Lark, risen like an angel
for the joy of a new dawning;
a lovely, gentle motion on
wings of song at our own
Earth Mother's bidding;
Nature, a treasure to behold
though it bring grief as well as joy;
Mother love, a gentle tale told
at bedtime - like a quilt
to keep us warm

Though we be orphans
in a storm

LOGON
(For Shaun)

Hands reaching out
across time, space;
Offers of friendship
in a kinder place;
Flames in the heart
licking at a screen;
Words, making a start
at what we mean;
Fingers on the keys
getting it together;
Soulmates, at ease
with each other;
A pooling of minds
on why we're here;
(An opening of blinds
on who we are?);
Each day as it comes,
making waves;
One to one, surfing
cyberspace

LINES ON FRIENDSHIP
(For Liz)

Out of nowhere you came,
pleasantly disturbing my day,
hauntingly reworking
my clay;
Time was, we were young
on a school trip to Paris
as cool as landing
on the moon;
Drawn together by chance,
romance a sweet illusion
thrown into upbeat
confusion;
How naïve I was then,
about women, about men,
about life, love – and
who I am!
You, a spirited ambience
easy on the ear - and
I shed a tear
for us;
No ships passing by night,
but aspects of youth
seeking truth – and
finding out;

No matter that we're grey
or I'm gay, our lives
like loose ends
in a play

At each Strutting Hour's end
no fretting time with a friend

A COMPANY OF PLAYERS

Everyday faces
in everyday places
making do with the weather
and other wild goose chases
after rainbows, pots of gold,
fairy tales told in schools
taking kids for fools,
about part-time jobs
on full-time pay,
Age of Leisure
here to stay

Painted devils, on
High Street walls.

CHALK AND CHEESE

We met at a party and I recall thinking
how loudmouths should refrain
from drinking;
When my turn came for a corny chat-up
line, dissuading took a discreet
knee in the groin;
At my home the next day, flowers
arrived - that I
ignored;
Next, a call with grovelling apologies
asking for a date, the
cheek of it!
Without making too many analogies
with a Mad Hatter's do, the
meal was a fiasco;
We kept tripping over our tongues
and, finally, took refuge
in silence;
Imagine my surprise when I took a call
suggesting a repeat
performance!
This time, we almost enjoyed a picnic
with champagne - until it
poured with rain;
I forget how many times we agreed
never to see each other
again

At least life was never boring. I even
learned to live with the snoring

A JOY FOREVER

When I am with you,
the world seems a better place
by far. I frame your face
in tender hands (no need to
catch a falling star)
and all my wishes come true;
My life with you is blessed
(I knew that time we kissed
after a mad dash
in pouring rain, and missed
the last bus home);
My dream is yours, the future.
ours to savour, like
a subtle flavouring of herbs
in the plainest fare;
No greater thrill, ever, than
our arms homing in
upon each other, warmth
like a dove's down
filling us, your lips like petals
waking to a glorious
new dawn, whispering
a first love story
of our own,
hearts beating
as one

LOVE FOR SALE

Mirror, mirror, on the wall
observe the gall of a man
regarding a gaudy shirt on display
that's slim fitting and trendy
(he, stout and grey);
Watch the hard mouth crease
(he plainly sees the joke);
Head in a rare spin as a shop
assistant goes into the old routine;
Moves on in a pleasant dream,
inner eye contemplating a wild thing,
mortgaged now to wife and kids
and probably happier than
he deserves…
Going back to buy the shirt
for a wild son, forgiven
thinking the old man's
gone bananas

MAKING A DIFFERENCE

Will some fallen angel
pick on me and drag
me away?
Or will a gentler spirit
have mercy, come
Judgement Day?
Shall wolfish death
delight in tearing
us apart...
or will it strike swift
and cleanly, at
the heart?
May doves defy infernal
dark, fly eternal
light...
or, brought to earth,
stay out of mind,
out of sight?
Not ours to know
the how, where,
or when...
but of our kinder selves,
glad to give
and learn...
unite in Peace and Love
than passively wait
Death's turn...
though our leaders
make an endgame
of commonsense

We can make a difference

SECRETS

Sat on a beach,
watching the waves
roll in...out...and
back again - like
your feelings
for me

Just out of reach,
waiting for your love
to roll in…out...and
back again, like
mixed-up prose
and poetry

Whispering hearts
that dare not sing aloud
rolling in…out...and
back again, like
a summer rain
cloud

Sat on a beach,
longing to let our love
come together, like
flotsam, jetsam - for
any beachcomber
to discover

Be tide and love eternal,
we are but mortal

BEHIND BARS

We saw a dragon at the zoo
as tame as tame could be;
I swear it poked a tongue at you
and flashed a flame at me;
Sad eyes glowing like balls of fire
rained down on us like a shower
of meteors as we marvelled
at its powerful jaws and shiny scales
in various rainbow hues, weaving
fairy tales from distant lands
as we stood, holding hands
but didn't go too near as you can
never be too sure (even at a zoo)
that a dragon won't try and
get the better of you;
As we watched, it wagged
the tip of a giant tail as if to say
"Come again another day."
And its belly rolled a minor roar,
shaking every bar of its cage,
curling every page of our history,
scant regard for magic or mystery,
driving home a cruel reality.
On the outside, looking in - pale
imitation of a dragon

We looked at each other, gave
a sigh, caught out in a lie

GRANDAD*

Just a few lines to say …
a very Happy Birthday - and
how much you mean to me
though I might not always say
how I feel (not too good with
the spoken word here) but
never more sincere than now;
You've always been there
for me so I want you to know
it's meant everything...
and you're really
something

Just a few lines to say...
a very Happy Birthday - and
how much I admire you
for all you've been through
and your generation, but always
making time to see, hear, listen,
regardless of time, age, place;
a kind face - inviting a cruel world
to talk, walk, laugh, be happy;
and when we're feeling low...
a certain smile
on show

Just a few lines but true;
Grandad, I love you

*A young man contacted me on the Internet and asked if I would write a
poem for his grandad's birthday. I have slightly edited the original – for
grandads everywhere.

ART LOVERS

Leafy sky, Picasso blue
mocking us where we lie
drenched with life's sweeter dew
for thinking, you and I
that we are young again
before Time began, and
our long haul through
the killing fields
of Pan

Mock on. No finer art
touches the heart

ANGEL AT MY SHOULDER

When I'm lonely, you're the angel
at my shoulder;
When the going gets rough
I take my strength from you;
You're my joy and inspiration
in everything I do;
I loved you from the start.
When you gave me change
for the telephone, I gave you
back - my heart

When I'm hurting,
angel at my shoulder,
you're the one who soothes
this savage breast;
Time and time again,
you ease my pain;
For all I've so screwed up
in life - forget the rest;
Angel at my shoulder,
you're the best

If I'm happy,
angel at my shoulder,
it's only because I know
you're always there;
If I ever treat you badly,
it's a madness of the soul
crept up on me;
For eternity I'm yours,
and swear it's true,
I love you too

WORLD CINEMA

Spread on a coat,
hands on hips,
watching clouds
like movie clips;
A coming together
of shadows,
words unfamiliar,
world cinema;
Two fingers touch,
marking a twin
celebration, cautious
anticipation;
Main feature, re-make
of a classic,
better left well alone
for television?

Clouds, camera, action

SPRING FEVER

We greeted love
on a high, my heart and I,
acting our parts sublime
for beech, sycamore, lark, nightingale,
lured by Nature's call
though sure to ignore
the cuckoo's
yell

On secret beaches
we scooped up sunshine
in fractured eye;
each caress, each kiss, a promise
wrung to madness
as highest tides
swept
us

We abandoned love
without thinking, seduced by
the smiles on gay faces
in crowd places starting to spread
everywhere, till finally
reduced to haunting
someone else's
nest

THE SECRET GARDEN

Mouth on mine
devouring this lonely heart,
imploring me to start
living again, forget we
were strangers in the rain
exchanging glances
in a shop window, reflecting
on missed chances,
non-starter romances;
Hands on my body
driving down lonely avenues,
exploring secret gardens
blooming with flowers,
fruits of summer showers
and lonely hours kept
keeping busy rather than
let feelings of intimacy
get the better of me;
A native sexuality
more a part of me than
hand thrust in glove,
whose familiarity brings
a warmth and sensuality
words dare not explain
any more than strangers
seeking to come in
from the rain;

Penetrating the silence
of my soul, a driving
force I never thought to
know again, bringing
truth and life to my secret
garden, songbirds singing
Nature's celebration
of perfect harmony,
you and me.

No sex more splendid
than love's first seed.

ODE TO MY LOVE

I love you for the smile
on your lips, the laughter
in your eyes, the way your hair
blows in a summer breeze,
how tears fall like a gentle rain
from heaven whenever we
watch soap television;
I love you for the song
in your heart, how it echoes
all around, sweeter sound even
than skylark or nightingale
lifting my soul on wings
of prayer given thanks
for your being here;
I love how you flare
like a candle in the wind
whenever we quarrel, making
up before the day closes,
recharging our bodies,
the more joy and power
to each other;
I love you for the way
you carry sorrow, brave and true
when life turns not as it seems;
though it tread roughly on
our dreams, you'll take
my hand, reassure - who
could ask for more?

HOLD THE DREAM

Met at a dance, got into romance
later, summer moon as misty
as a priest's glass eye,
voices in the wind
making us laugh,
making us cry;
Evening star, a light in the eye;
World ceasing to turn,
one moment supreme;
Voices in the wind
sighing "Yes"- to
our first kiss;
Never a night like this!
Heaven, like a loving parent
bound to keep on smiling
and reassuring - though
voices in the wind,
a mixed blessing;
Come dawn, rejoicing;
A tumble of clowns ringing
in the ears as we take our places
at the Circus of Life, playing
down our fears, rising above
lonely years

PARTY PIECES

He gatecrashed
a private party,
caused a stir,
left early;
Looked like a poster
on my wall, even
the toothpaste
smile;
Colourful, sleek
as fame,
playing the name
game;
Homing in on
a hung lip,
soaking up hero
worship;
Like lovers, dancing
cheek to cheek,
drowning in world
music;
Soon, speeding
dark streets,
intent on usurping
lark sheets;
Me, I went home,
tore him down,
in pieces slept
alone

MAKING HISTORY

Castle of the skin
risen proud and tall,
let the world in

Through thick and thin,
good and evil,
castle of the skin

Declare the doors open,
(enemy at the wall?)
let the world in

Ask neighbours to dine
in the ancestral hall,
castle of the skin

Our joy and salvation,
no empty shell,
let the world in

Men, women, children,
be a credit to us all;
Castle of the skin,
let the world in

JUST GOOD FRIENDS?

Wanting to love you
but did not dare;
Wanting to tell you
but afraid - of what
I might hear;
Wanting to let you see
how it hurt me;
Caring, sharing just
about everything
but honesty;
Trying to concentrate
on being a mate
while lusting after
your body - day
and night;
Each time we part,
an aching heart,
until the next time
we meet - and it
takes flight;
Dying to lay the truth
on your mouth,
let the world hear a
song - caged bird
of my youth;
How to express this
love I suppress,
risk my dreams falling
apart at the seams, our
world collapse?

In tears, I confessed,
expecting the worst;
You replied with a grin
as your heart let me in
and at last...

We kissed

OLD HAUNTS

World's reflection
in bedsit windows
seeking companions
on street corners

Cracks on a pane
like shattered dreams
made whole again
when the sun shines

Lonely, a sad word
like early autumn mist
beguiling our world
like a friendly ghost

*Treading hopefully
through eternity*

PLEASE, LISTEN

You lay your head on my shirt
listening to my heart;
Does it tell you all the things
I long to say – but can never
find the words?
Do you hear a love song
stolen from the birds?
Don't you know I need you
more than I can show?
No? Then listen, let my heart
tell you so

We were made for one another;
Soulmates forever, sharing
life, love, dreams - looking out
for each other when Hope
falls apart at the seams;
Passion's heat, no smouldering
hearth - but electric shards
charging the earth in a summer
storm. Can't you hear?
No? Then listen, let my heart
tell you so

WORLD WITHOUT END

The sea, the sea
reminisces me;
Shapes, sounds, swell;
The two of us playing,
children in the sand,
making waves, marking well
teasing limbs, keeping time
with ice cream
chimes

The sea, the sea
braves me;
Shapes, sounds, swell;
The two of us lying,
lovers in the sand,
making waves, marking well
each nuance of flesh
consuming us, gulls
crying

The sea, the sea,
you, me;
Shapes, sounds, swell;
Camera's on children
playing in the sand,
making waves; lovers marking
well our castles in the air,
once-upon-a-time world
to share

WOODLANDERS

Memories, dancing on
the skin, like a gypsy
tambourine;
The two of us making love
on a battered
trench coat;
Swallows nesting above
with concerns of
their own
though, unlike ours,
answerable
to none;
Earth's music, a glorious
symphony, dying notes
no tragedy
though we can but
snatch at
Time
with child hands delighting
in the picking
of bluebells,
applauding the first
flight of baby
swallows,
sharing Nature's rapture
forever to
endure;
To the sweet smelling earth
ourselves freely
given

PART THREE

GAY'S THE WORD

GAY'S THE WORD

On vacation in New York
they called me a fag
and I shrivelled up inside;
On the streets of Brixton
someone yelled, "He's queer!"
(just like my dad);
Guys in a bar cried, "homo!"
because I wore a ribbon
with pride;
Some of the women at work
got lewd - about a waste
of manhood;
I felt a clammy mist closing
in on me, unsure what
to do...
till someone said "Hey,
I hear your gay?
Me too..."
And the warmth of a grin
let the sun
back in

THE TWO OF US

Under Paris stars, one night
in June - a nightingale
sang our tune;
We embraced, exchanging
vows - with tongues
of fire;
No chill of darkness
intruding upon
our happiness;
You put your hand in mine.
To each other, a ring - meant
everything;
Come morning, sweet night
kissed us each, a fond
au'revoir;
Minute's silence- for
two singles joined
together;
Cock crows as we embrace
a parallel dawn - bask
in its glory;
Story told, the world
over - me and my
gay lover

CAPITAL GAY

Pull up a chair in a busy café,
loll there, blond hair
gone grey;
Sun setting on us, covers
the head - like
a pink beret;
Thunder in the ears, years
of acid rain rimming
the century;
Nine-to-five heroes passed on,
leaving V-signs on the
stationery;
Pages of patched-up history
like penises
erect;
Victory, sheer curiosity
for the politically
correct

Hail-fellow-well-met, on
Old Compton Street

BALLAD OF THE BOY NEXT DOOR

I used to play at cowboys
with the boy next door;
We'd walk to school together,
share the homework chore;
Later we went to discos
and danced all night...
got drunk, tried drugs, began
to drift apart

I missed him more than words
can ever say,
having grown to love him
in such a way...
a smile that beat a roll of drums
on my heart,
playful touches like matches
to my shirt

Eventually, I knew, I must
make a decision;
I packed us in a box - marked
Do Not Open...
along with cowboy hats
and school reports;
Mad, musical days long gone
as life goes on

We met up again in a bar
one day;
I had one too many, told him
I'm gay;
His eyes filled with tears,
and I sensed distain...
as my tongue ran away
with years of pain

Afterwards, I dashed out
in the rain…
spent hours, wishing we were
cowboys again;
He found me in a dingy
back street café,
his hair a mess, face lined
and grey

I didn't want to hear what
he had to say…
but the look in his eyes
made me to stay;
Could it be, I wondered,
that he understood?
Then I knew for sure
he did

*Fingertips touching, like
lovers kissing*

WIN SOME, LOSE SOME

We got raunchy in a sauna
but didn't get very far;
People kept interrupting
and we weren't up for
an orgy;
So we drove into the country,
had sex among the trees,
birds nesting above
us, as snug as
you please;
Our bodies kindled one another
like newspaper to a flame,
pledged each other
half truths - until
dawn;
We woke, passion faded
like the moon,
got real and went home;
I didn't ask his number
or give mine

We both knew there wouldn't
be a next time

MAKING HEADLINES

Let the rain at me, a lusty wind!
Smelly yellow of a shopping bag
spilling me over;
Beating off politicos, press,
sightseers - with Persephone's
umbrella;
Down, down a side street,
deadpan god in a leather jacket
jostling;
Adrenalin flowing;
(Could be a pickpocket, worse?
I knew, of course);
Chanced a glance, glimpsed
a jerk of tousled head;
Aroused, followed where he led,
a roomy cottage, gloomy as Hades;
Groped each other excitedly,
over too quickly;
He ran off, left me pleading
with a policeman leaning on my arm
for job, reputation...
asking, "Where's the harm?"
But fingers stroking a truncheon
refused to listen;
Charged at the station, strip
searched - for whatever;
Brought to court, lectured on
anti-social behaviour;
Fined more than a drunk driver
for manslaughter

REFUGEE

Persecuted for being gay
in another country,
he smuggled himself away,
became newsworthy

The tabloids went to town
and TV took up the fight
against that country's violation
of Human Rights

Local councils argued a while
about where a single gay man
should be housed; after all,
can't please everyone

Captured by a nation's heart,
lover refused a passport

TALKING HEADS

One finger brushes my hand
as if wanting me to understand
all your eyes long to convey
though you dare not look
up from your book...
as your lips half shape
what they will not say
because you've not yet
learned the words for
feelings gay

I let my leg press yours,
feel scalding tremors
pulse through our bodies
like an electric shock...
yet you will not look
up at me but lick your lips
nervously, swallowing
the taste of me, coming to
terms with an enduring
curiosity

I let my gaze caress your face,
on sensual mouth place
a gentle kiss, full lips parting
to let my tongue explore...
not reading any more (if you
ever were). Though heads, noses,
ears, rush us from all sides
like attitudes...keep fiddling
with that shirt button, it's
a lifeline

Together, against
the Hydra

CYBERNETICS

IM'ing the screen bluntly,
may be an invasion of privacy
but there's such a thing
as curiosity - and if it killed
the cat, so what?
Give or take a white lie or two,
CKs on cue - cyber invention
promoting a predilection
for erection @ a/s/l.com
(age, sex, location);
"So, what turns you on?"
You deliver, expect likewise
but the devil plays clever
and demands
your size...
Not up for all that,
prefer to chat, play IT by ear?
Invariably, they'll choose
"Ignore"- cruise other meets
for better invites

Reality bytes

A SUMMER STORM

Heart as heavy
as clouds hanging low;
Soul struck dumb
by lightning flashes
of disillusion;
Rain on the face
compensating for tears
unshed, while trying
face up to your leaving
without a word;
Your last kisses
like honey on the tongue;
Bee without a hive
or reasons to weather
a summer storm;
Weary and wet,
sadly heading home;
Sun comes out
and birds start to sing,
children shouting;
I see you waiting
on the doorstep, drenched,
shoulders hunched;
Storm over. Still raining.
New beginning?
Time enough
for questions, answers
or finding words;
Let our tears
reunite us

Gay lovers

COPS, QUEERS AND CARAVAGGIO

We met in an art gallery,
enjoyed each other's company
all day;
At his flat, we chatted over
coffee and, finally, he asked me
to stay;
Although both nervous,
we made love, the two of us
in heaven...
nor just having fun;
Good to be close to someone
again;
His mouth, warm and sensual;
An embrace far more than sexual
wanting me...
as more than a friend
but no mere means to an end
physically;
He brought me breakfast
in bed and I turned a shade red
at his uniform;
I hadn't asked about
his career, content just to be there
with him...
so it came as a shock
to see him dressed as a P.C.
for the beat;
Tried to tell myself
it didn't matter, heart all a-flutter
and cold feet;

At the door, a shy goodbye,
copper's shirt and tie a brick
wall...
that crumbled with an embrace
as we saw, face to face, nothing
mattered at all

Lovers till he moved away;
Friends to this day.

LIP SERVICE

They asked if I was married,
I had to answer no;
Did I have a girlfriend,
a partner - or perhaps
I was a widower?
I'm gay, I said, so what?
It mattered not a jot,
they hastily assured me,
it's the 21st century

They went off to a party
without inviting me.

POINTS OF VIEW

It won't do to be gay,
you said;
It won't do at all,
whatever...
People may pretend
not to mind...
but most prefer the company
of their own kind;
It could ruin your
Life forever;
Better play safe...
Take on a wife and semi,
raise kids, bash away
at Promotion's door, keep
the neighbours happy;
Discover (for sure?) how
acting "normal" hypes
a higher dividend
than throwing in with
gay types – to the
bitter end;
Equal Ops, a revolution
but same sexes at the altar
and adoption - hardly
a proper option

Points of view, certainly,
but you're you, I'm me.

A GOOD SIGN

White tee, blue eyes
cruising a crowded bar,
glances around
as he orders;
Settles on green eyes
lit with the kind of smile
an angel would
die again for;
Crosses to sit nearby
and shyly nods a 'hello'
but - no reply, so
gets up to go;
Green Eyes, running
fingers through blond hair,
full lips pursed, exposing
a hairy chest...
stretches a downy leg
in lycra shorts, Blue slowly
drowning in the wildest
thoughts;
"I'm deaf," he says
in the queerest voice,
making up his mind,
staking a choice;
Blue grins, winks,
signs that he also wants
some action
for once;
Among lonely hearts
in a crowded Soho dive,
two pairs of hands
come alive

TWO'S COMPANY

Met a girl at a coffee bar
and we got chatting;
Her boyfriend joined in
the fun;
Hair as black as his leather
jacket, faded 501's;
As we talked and laughed
all three;
His hand, under our table,
touched my knee;
It meant nothing, I felt
fairly sure;
My whole body, suddenly
on fire;
She kept cracking jokes
that made us roar;
A finger brushing mine,
I could not ignore,
dangling me on a fence
of barbed wire;
I kept my eyes on
his snub nose;
Bright eyes, wide grin ripping
off my clothes;
Madly, I let him explore
my all;
Gladly, surrendered
body and soul;
Imagined my hand tucked in
his shirt, thrilling to
the frantic rhythm
of his heart;
They left hand in hand.

I sat alone, stunned;
On my third decaf
he returned;
No words to explain how
or why;
Getting a grip on our
sexuality;
Four hands on a table, still
visibly shaking
from an incredible
lovemaking;
He told me his name,
handshake firm
and it was like
coming home

YESTERDAY MAN

I used to wonder if I'm really gay
till I saw him on the beach one day,
blond hair bleached by the sun,
blue eyes laughing at everyone,
a smile that ran up and down my spine,
lips I'd rather taste than wine,
a body so trim and tight,
I fell for him at first sight
and it felt right

I had a hard on every day
that summer holiday;
At night, we'd make love
in the wildest dreams,
bodies joined with such warmth
and passion, I couldn't believe
a conversation I overheard
about poufs, queers, shirt lifters
and pervs

I contrived to crash into him,
let his beauty enter me with all
the ecstasy of a fruit flavoured
condom and his voice seduce me
out of my shell. Hadn't I been
in hell for ages - haunted, taunted
by questions of sexual identity?
Well, here was an angel
sent to answer me!

I guessed he was straight,
and wouldn't have dared say
a word. Besides, I was scared.
One day, in the water,
he accused me of staring
and I blushed to the roots
of my hair. He just laughed
and pulled me down - till
I thought I'd drown!

I thrashed and fought, like a fish
caught on a line, but he soon
calmed me down with a grin
though I all but panicked again
as his arms held me close
and the sea told me, "Yes!"
Nor did he have in mind a mere
race to the shore - we
both wanted more

Seems like only yesterday, I used
to wonder if I'm really gay

EARLY MORNING DIP

He lay next to me
breathing quietly;
Pecs under his tee
like crests of wavelets
on a balmy sea;
Blue shorts, teasing me
like summer skies
fluffing up for rain
maybe

Hairy legs, tickling me
like a summer breeze;
Flesh, a comfort
of hot sand on
my belly, as I snuggle
close - and we
let the sea
take us

*Breaststrokes, before
breakfast*

RUNNING TRUE

We chat for a while
and walk apace
while fluffy bits start
to gather, wipe the
sweet smile from
heaven's face

Pause under a willow's
weepy awning, ponder
killing off a desperate
yearning for each other
on the spot - but
cannot

Such tears for the death
of innocence, falling
like spring rain!
Like a river, blood
running faster
in the vein

Storm warning false,
heaven at ease with
the day again;
Fluffy bits on the river
like wreaths, floating
in the sun

Snug inside the willow,
your heart for
a pillow;
Feted by a lark, giving
Nature's belated
blessing

Spring days, running
true - for gays too

PULP FICTION

He got on at Leicester Square,
sat opposite me, heading
for Edgware;
Between dripping sardines
our eyes met. (Rain on the face
or beads of sweat?)
I chanced a friendly smile
and mouthed
"Hello."
He flung me a dirty look - so
I returned to my book
although my heart
yearned for his beauty,
let it comfort
my despair;
Oh, to burn my fingers
on the sparklers
in his hair!
Patched jeans, smouldering
like the heart cowering
in my shirt;
I risked a second glance.
His eyes bore darkly
into mine;
Hooked! And starkly,
we swam a glorious
ocean;
Our lovemaking done
by Camden Town,
he left the train

I never saw him again

FIGHTING TALK

We'd quarrelled
and I wanted no truck
with you, wouldn't
make it up with you;
I took the spare bed,
wondering what's going on
in your head, other side
of the wall, were you
thinking of me
at all?

At last I slept,
only to be woken roughly,
duvet torn off me,
merging mouths closing
in on eternity;
Eyes shining, blood rushing
to the war cries of angels
fighting over
our rights to
a blessing

If they won't marry us,
let 'em bury us

EYES WIDE SHUT

Met an ugly man in a trendy bar
and confess, I wondered
what he was doing there;
We got chatting and after a while
I realised he had
a lovely smile;
His gentle voice, a musical lilt
that sent me falling
full tilt;
He offered a hand, told me his name;
His touch was electric
as I returned mine;
His conversation was fun
(no boring small talk
or chat-up line);
He winked and asked me shyly
if I'd like to come back
for a coffee;
Later, sex as pure art form
filling my lonely soul
with such passion...
as I'd never known before,
this ugly-beautiful man
in a trendy bar

Colluding with the heart,
eyes wide shut

BURN-OUT

You were sitting alone
with a beer, green eyes
everywhere, sunlight
in reddish hair like sparks
from a winter fire that lit
a flame in my heart
from the start;
I wanted to speak - but
did not dare in case
you sent me packing
with a flea in my ear
so I hung around,
and tried to pretend
I was with a friend;
You glanced my way,
piercing my heart,
played with a button
on your shirt...
I glimpsed a tawny hair
as a twinkle in the eye
beckoned me near;
We chatted awhile, your
smiling face arousing
such heat in me that
you were a part of me
long before we finally
came together, at
your place

Desire fulfilled, phone
numbers filed

A GAY DAD'S STORY
(For Don)

Married, with kids, and not unhappy,
lives all but running true;
Trying to be a good husband, dad,
seems the right thing to do;
Of daily life, real love no less a part
for phantoms tugging at the heart, like
children longing to come out to play
but made to stay indoors, lest angels
with dirty faces lower the tone,
heaven looking on

Married, with kids, and not unhappy,
lives all but running true;
Trying to be a good husband, dad,
seems the right thing to do;
Few greater joys of Mother Earth
than love, togetherness and birth;
Nor do these fade, though others
burst through like spring flowers,
a long, hard winter done,
heaven looking on

Parted, kids grown, and not as happy
as we ought to be;
But a sense of integrity, worthy
of our sexuality;
Time enough for friends and family
to understand, lessons learned,
no love, once freely given,
completely overturned;
Same sun duly rising,
heaven cheering

ODE TO A FLY

One beautiful day
I chanced where he lay
and my heart filled
with music but my feet
refused to follow, else
the vision go away
and leave me feeling
oh, so hollow!

Three shirt buttons
were undone, a hairy chest
tickling my spine;
One hand stroked a mane
of hair, spread like sand
on the grass; the other
taking care of a fly
on his shorts

Zap! Fly caught.
But, what's this? Set free
by a caring hand that blew
a kiss, beckoned me…
although I knew he could
not see where I hid, like
a spy – full of envy
for a fly

I emerged, strolled
by leisurely, not daring
to trust a glance, till you
called to me laughingly
and asked my heart
to dance – and a lark
sang for us, my
first waltz

Like a fly, caught and freed;
Only, I stayed

GONE FISHING

There was a fishing hole
down our way;
I used to go there
every day;
Didn't fish for perch
or go for trout;
Didn't need a rod, or
use bait;
Reeling in dreams
one, two three...
Tall, slim and dark
(smiling, carefree);
Game for a lark, beneath
a friendly willow tree
conspiring with summer
to draw us closer...
till we dared to kiss
under leafy skies

No more lies

PAPERBACK WRITER

Walking in the park...
saw you lying on the grass
eyes closed, face turned
to the sun – and thought
I had never seen such beauty
in anyone;
Sat down nearby...
trying hard not to look,
began to read a book
upside down - peering over
its faded cover, at
my dream lover;
Later, we chatted...
my heart skipping beats
like a lamb for the joys
of spring – in the sunshine
of your smile, grateful
just for living;
Too soon, we parted...
as your hand in mine, firm
and strong, carried me
to heaven - on the wings
of a favourite
pop song;
Gone separate ways...
I tumbled back to earth
as blue as my novel's
paper cover – dreaming
a happy ending, with
each other;
A backward glance...
unable to resist a wistful
look – nor could you
but ran back too, helped me
write the best chapters
in my book

FOR A LOST SOLDIER

Once, summer tapped
me on the shoulder,
murmured in my ear
and when I turned
I saw a soldier – in
full gear

Asked the way to heaven
knows where - but I hardly
caught a word as the full
curve of his mouth
cut me deeper than
a sword

Voice teasing, haunting
eyes like an owl's
ripping at my clothes,
baring the soul as I
surrendered
my all

A woman took his arm,
smiled with all the charm
of Eve at Adam's side;
But the soldier winked
as they moved on
and I sighed

He hadn't lied

ANY OTHER MIDNIGHT

No bells ring out a year's passing
for us, just voices haunting
rims of glasses, the way
a zest for life taunts shadows
fallen across paper tigers
cruising hot lips;
Auld acquaintance, a
sleeping beauty

Peace Be

Dance. Let cynics wrinkle
a nose or two that never knew
how sweet the smell of leather
in a smoky room, hot flesh
taking the rise of torch-like eyes
among those sized up
and found wanting, by
a would-be lover

Starting over

BUS FARE

He was a very ordinary guy,
with an ordinary face,
wearing ordinary clothes;
I couldn't place why he stood
out from the crowd,
he just did

Fair, wavy hair that never
saw a dye; a hint of twinkle
in the eye, probably a lie
and never meant
to be read - the
way I did

When the seat next to him
became free, I sat down,
and would have engaged
in light conversation;
Instead, we both stared
straight ahead

He brushed against me
as he left the bus;
For a while, he was just
a Thought for the Day
till I got off, turned back,
ran all the way

*Caught up with his smile,
no ordinary guy at all*

TEA FOR TWO

Stirring my tea, brooding
about life, wishing things
different;
Less strife, angst, despair;
More hope and love
everywhere;
Suddenly, a hand took mine,
"You're spilling
your tea!"
I looked up, glaring
and found myself
staring....
into eyes as blue
as a picture postcard sea
and all I could do
was grin, foolishly
and try to
ignore...
nipples pricking his shirt,
making ripples down
my spine...
a lump in the throat,
full lips teasing
mine...
with a smile like the sun
on a cloudy day, come
out to play;
I let him wrap me in velvet,
pocket my dreams
in his jeans;
We left, tea unfinished,
still holding
hands

SHIPMATES

It was just a one-night stand,
I'd tell myself;
Mustn't let a fun time in bed
go to the head;
Get a grip. Stiff upper lip
and all that;
Read a book. Watch a movie.
Go for a walk, anything!
Must stop hovering, waiting for
the damn phone to ring, it won't.
But here I am, because it might.
Oh, we ships in the night!
(Logo for a tee shirt, bought
in Old Compton Street);
Chin up, chest out - time
to get real again, strut and fret
a Happy Hour, let some beer
take the strain

Away all boats, away

I flung open the door - and
there you were

GOING TO MEET THE MAN

A young man went to heaven,
and knocked at the door;
An angel came, looked him over,
told him he'd have to wait
a wee longer;
A second angel came along
carrying the Book,
scratched his head, giving
the man a hard,
old-fashioned look;
When a third angel arrived,
the youth managed to say,
'Is there a problem 'cause I'm gay?'
The angels muttered piously
'Truth will have its way.'
The young man broke down
but, turning to leave,
Someone took him gently
by the sleeve, saying
loud and clear

Who seeks, shall enter

PART FOUR

CHILDREN OF THE CENTURY

ENTER, THE MILLENNIUM

One man relaxes in the cabin
of a luxury yacht;
One man crouches under a wall
(it's all he's got);
One man glances from a porthole
at the sun going down;
One man watches a rat hole
with a serious frown;
The sun descended, one man
eats his fill;
The waiting ended, one man
makes a kill

WESTMINSTER, FIRST LIGHT

Heaven, trying
to shake us
awake;
Deadbeats coming
alive, like home
fires

Dawn, killing
off wishing
stars;
Lark, rising
above our
lies

CHILDREN OF THE CENTURY

Wandering dark tunnels,
lost and afraid;
Regulation torch for company,
imitation fur for the cold;
Batteries running low,
heartbeats erratic;
Which way to go?
(Hard, not to panic);
Where there's life, there's hope
or so they say;
Live to fight another day?
Brave words – when the Dark
is rising, Styx threatening
to burst its banks;
Press on, negotiating
all infernal terrors;
Pinpricks of light - comedy
of our errors, played
out to the end;
Look. Listen. See.
Hear rescuers descend?
Faith, Hope, Charity,
round the next bend
reappearing...

Children of the Century
found wanting

NO HIGHWAY

We tread a long, lonesome road,
my sometime shadow and I,
sharing a burdensome load,
weary of waiting to die

O, Death, be a friend to us
and travel our direction;
Pause and put an end to this
daily crucifixion

Long since abandoned here,
once such a time we had!
Mates, music, promising career
till the good life went bad

We took a wrong turn,
my sometime shadow and I,
chasing a friendly dragon
through a needle's eye

Ways open, ways close.
Dragon's jaws

GONE SHOPPING

Lonely heart cries out
like a bagged pup dropped
in a wishing well,
left to drown in the soul;
Is anybody there?
Does anyone hear, with
a wish to spare for us?
Pup, whining pitifully;
Heart, struggling bravely
to cease its freefall
in a shopping mall;
Voices. Words. Faces.
Eyes, mouths on the go...
like crowds pouring out
of a West End show, its star
taken ill suddenly and
a poor understudy;
Waste of money buying up
what no one wants, and
puppy mix costs a packet;
Wishes for a lottery win
falling like shooting stars
above the racket;
Shopper finds a corner
to curl up and let the world
wash over;
No one spots a body bag
for tossing coins
in the water

GODS AND MONSTERS

Deep in the heart of me
a part you'll never see
yearns to be forever free
of native ties that bind;
Door on the world slams tight,
bolts dragged shut;
Bats' wings like swords
penetrating words the mind
cannot suppress, lips
never converse;
Stirring, horror and tongues
of fire beneath layer upon layer
of sheer profanity;
The world's inhumanity,
(for how long put down
by our spirituality?) - feeding
on its very temporality;
Voices, like an angel choir
colouring the heart's desire
whatever it takes

Kraken wakes

GETTING A LIFE

Fled their own country,
hunted down there
like foxes to the lair
for supporting democracy
in the face of conspiracy
and fraud among mandarins
of power (public ambitions,
masks for hypocrisy);
Left friends, family, home
for a future among people
who'll surely welcome
such as they? Hopeful...
that any dignity torn
from humanity prove
reparable

ARENA

As a hungry lion will champ
on human bones - so
a consummate bestiality
has the world in its grip;
Man against man;
Woman against woman;
Men and women vying
with each other, for superiority
over a jungle mentality?
Our children masturbating
for small comfort, emulating
the signs - survival
of the fittest;
Watch the world's physicians,
take a lead, thumbs at
the ready - playing
to the crowd;
Gladiators, spectators
all eager to feed
and beating at
the breast

Enter, a pride of lions
to the contest

DANCING WITH NIETZSCHE

Bright lights, dark sound
all around;
Wish I could see your face,
obscured by pink lace;
Wonder, are you frowning at me
or drowning too, slowly?
Wish you could see my face,
obscured by pink lace;
New boots drag me down,
pink and blue sea...
the wonder of this place
spreading, shining faces
beckoning me on, our
reckoning all but done,
now gathering pace
in pink lace;
White tee, jeans,
swam with the fishes,
finally surfaces;
And might I see
who brought me to this?
Re-writing history,
penetrating time, space,
pink lace

BATTLE LINES?

Asian, black, white young people
expressing frustration, not least
with Society's perpetration
of lip service to
integration;
Equal Ops, well-intentioned
policy; political correctness,
clever diplomacy and
whatever happened
to honesty?;
Sex, sexuality, colour creed...
our individuality, a need
to preserve but not at
any cost - or the war
already lost;
Racial identity, no ready sword
to hurt for hurting's sake,
defying harmony - along
lines of cultural
bigotry;
Let's turn to Peace and Love,
spurn taboos and other
"No-go" areas, learn
from history's
battle scars

Or bury our dead, rivers
of blood

NATIONAL CURRICULUM

Today we have history
and World War Two
spills across the room,
filling every trench, with
a stench of homesickness
and blood, desks dripping
pools of mud, where
elbows nudge each other;
Half an eye on the clock
as we get stuck in

Under fire again

Bayonets fixed; wonder
if we'll have the guts
to use 'em? Somewhere,
birdsong and sunshine
but these have no place
in skies where Death's
own face pours acid tears
on a gung-ho, glory,
atomic bomb package
in bias text

Science next

OUT OF SIGHT, OUT OF MIND

Through smoky skies,
hear the cries of lost children
trudging the weary earth,
seeking reasons for their birth,
chasing seasons told about
in fairy tales, tucked up in bed
before sweet dreams take over;
Instead, left to live a nightmare,
grow old before their time,
nibbling at childhood, in
comfort-seeking corners
where sugar mice play
and slaves only see the light
of day to toil corporate
industry, slowly killing
themselves - to fill
our shelves

TAKING SIDES

Child of Africa
chanting in the sun,
following where
his father gone

Woman of Africa
dares shed a tear
for a family
at war

Man of Africa,
three out of three;
War, want,
dignity

People, wanting
to be heard;
Martyrs, to the colour
of our word

Portfolio waving
a black cab;
Now, there's
the rub

TALK OF THE DEVIL

Sometimes the Devil takes us,
children too, and makes us do
things we don't want to - but
little choice, led by the nose
despite our worst fears
through the world's
nightmares;
Sometimes the Devil leaves
his mark on a victim, chosen
at random to satisfy a craving
for evil - and we must live
with the death of Innocence,
no way of making
recompense;
Sometimes we put up a fight
and the Devil gladly takes
us on, Master of our nether
regions, likely to win against
any poor soul relying
on natural justice
to prevail;
Sometimes help is at hand,
though not always in time,
a chance to beat the Devil
at his own game; a light
in our darkness, pitting
Peace and Love against
his defences;

Pity the Devil's children
though a battle won, left
fighting others without
and within, not least the
right to live - in a world
finding it hard
to forgive;
Cry retribution for a small boy
left, mutilated, on a railway line
and let the Devil feed on our
pain - or salvation for a world
that insists on counting
the Devil's Children
among its own?

War zone

SECRETS AND LIES

In nether regions
of the mind, behind locked
doors of the soul, dwells
a demon with lean and hungry
look - as when I thrust it there
the day after it came for me
and first led me astray…
into ways I can but dwell upon
with fear and hellish scorn
but visit every day, let it feed
on flesh and bone, small price
to pay to keep well hid...
as stars fall down on each
lonely head left to face
Eternity - only demons
for company?

HOMEWORK

Photos by the bed,
posters on the wall,
press cuttings on a chair
likely to hit the floor
if someone opens
the door;
So the door stays shut,
keeping strangers out
while anxious faces debate
human rights, pollution,
nature conservation,
our salvation...
education, discrimination,
traffic congestion, political
correctness (on the face
of it), safer sex, drugs,
always having to
be alert;
Clamour of voices kicking
the soul, like a football
across the room;
Conscience, scoring
an own goal - now
and then;
Questions, answers, lies,
half lies, home truths
like moths to a light;
Please, someone, open
the door - and
let us out!

ON THE BEACH

Fighting for Right, against
a bitter tide of Wrong;
Sure to drown, who won't swim;
Waves crashing, a sound thrashing
for every mother's son and daughter
with neither grace nor favour;
No lambs to the slaughter,
but bold Surfers of History
denying old gods
a final victory

Riding life's highs and lows;
competing with friends, outwitting
our foes; God only knows why.
Waves cry out for war-war;
Surfers ignore, watchers on the shore
go for jaw-jaw and dog-paddles
while the world holds its breath
at the biggest show on earth;
Modernity, surfing
with irony

WINGS OF DESIRE

Humming sky, coming for me
like a sheet at bedtime;
Lying where willows still
whisper the fall
of Icarus

On Nature's pillow,
wet dreams of us;
Suspended by a Boeing 747
staking its claim
on heaven

You, me, dragon
flying high;
Caught out in lie after lie,
passing through
a needle's eye

Old god's still laughing
at a generation's
preoccupation with heaven,
hell, tongues of fire,
wings of desire

INSIDE

Can't hear for ghosts, scratching at
the door, damp patches on walls,
bars across a window taunting us
with good days, green spaces,
would-be faces;
Sweating like a sick kids on a hot day
who's ma won't let us out to play,
discovering new ways to get by
(must try, can't help
asking - why?);
Someone jokes, someone farts;
Broken sleep, broken hearts patched
up carefully; screams no one
will hear, tears no one
must see;
Puppets jerking to order except for
a pretty harmonica player making
precious little sense - of a world
losing its dignity, busy
scoring points;
Anaesthetized by a love-hate fix
that's all we cell mates exist for;
Deserving everything we get
or prisoners of conscience
and regret?
Ghosts, scratching at the door
but nothing to say we haven't
heard before, thought
couldn't hurt us
any more

Can't you hear?

BAG LADY

Taxpayers nudge one another
under the scrutiny of a hag squint;
She scowls at the daily round,
mutters a lot, picks her nose;
Always about, in sunshine or rain,
wrapped in a greatcoat;
Peers in our faces, for a view
of better times?
Plagued by school kids'
cruel rhymes;
Once seen queuing
at a bus stop

Fag end of society
bagging us up

SLEEPING IT OFF

We're a long time lying
in this earthy bed;
Weary limbs belie
an active mind;
Get up, sleepy head!
Closed eyes can't explore
the moon, nor a prayer
bring instant fortune;
Sheep count, too close
to call

Wakey-wakey, one
and all

WEEKENDS

Nothing, will ever come
of that potted dream,
lost sight of once Monday
takes shape;
Nothing will ever come
of those half plans
spread-eagled on a noon
sandwich;
Nothing will ever come
of chatting up
you-know-who at the next
big do;
Nothing, nothing at all
for daring to bare
the soul - in Sunday's
cold pew

Says who?

BEAT GENERATION

Spider in the corner,
pop star on the wall;
Icon beside the bed
casting tall enough
shadows to keep a spider
from harm and God
in the Top Ten;
Come into my parlour
says the spider to a fly,
hear my latest CD;
Let's relax, get high,
act our parts, put the world
to rights, rate God
in the charts;
On the black market,
could be a pirate, need
to take care;
Party Political Broadcast
puts the Devil just
about - everywhere,
who knows?
Never mind the words,
go where the music flows
for good or ill;
Backs to the wall, big smile!
C'mon, let's rock 'n' roll,
we saints, sinners, losers,
winners all

Cool

SHADOWS

Someone in the shadows
asked me...
I said "No!" Yet they followed
and sweet talked me,
broke my will - so
I bought the
damn pill

Someone in the shadows
begged me...
I said "No!" Yet they followed
and sweet talked me,
broke my will - so
I gave them the
damn pill

Someone in the shadows
told me...
I said "No!" Yet they followed
and bad mouthed me,
broke my will - but
I still went to the
funeral

*Shadows everywhere, bending
the ear*

ISLANDS

Drowning, in an office swim.
Clutching at straws as each new threat
of relocation puts the damper
on promotion;
Putting in unpaid overtime.
Pillow talk, levelled to a snore;
Partner, keeping
the score;
Can't relax and pills don't help.
Walking the dog offers small respite
from a long day's journey
into night;
A need to be held, a need to confide;
A need to feel safe, a place to hide;
Yet - for all we say, see, think,
feel, look...
Life's a closing book - once Man
bites dog, seals an imperfect spirituality?
So, let's write a fitting epilogue
to the comedy

Rush in where angels fear to tread
or share the load?

FIGURES IN A LANDSCAPE

Colours, plain enough to see,
tricks of light portraying
the same scene differently;
Inner eye, homing in
Selectively

Familiar enough backdrop;
Humanity, busy scrapping
hell-bent on settling old
scores under the noses
of our betters

Society stripped of dignity,
integrity open to question;
Hypocrisy ripped away
like ozone, the future
uncertain

Nature left to go it alone;
World conforming to tribal
identities, a conflicting
evolution; pictures in
an exhibition

THE HAUNTED HEART

Should have done more

Pictured, the tortured mind
and soul in slow free fall;
Sounds, like the creaking
of a kissing gate - where
we used to meet after school
and wonder what a God
would make of us all;
You were unhappy I could tell
(yet never easy to know for sure
when it's but imagination
knocking at the door
to be let in)

No word or sign signified
despair - until your suicide
kicked open my door

Should have done more

NO ORDINARY DAY

Getting ready for work,
going to school;
Chatting on the cell phone
how life's cool;
Taking a flight, just like
any other;
An ordinary day…
11th September;
Suddenly, hijacked!
Terror in the sky, cell phones
calling to say "I love you
though I die…"
Offices below, at the heart
of a nation, throbbing
the day-to-day business
of salvation;
Suddenly, struck!
Death, horror, confusion;
World ripped apart
on television;
Who can imagine the horror,
pain, despair? Only disbelief
that such a thing could
happen here;
Survivors and the dead…
victims of a terrorist outrage;
Rescue workers killed - for
their very courage;

Heroes inspiring faith, hope
and a will to overcome...
among the tears for thousands
never coming home;
Who knows where we go
from here? But let us pray
for Peace, not war - however
long it takes;
Though a bough break, cradle
fall on Ground Zero...
let there be songbirds in trees
and spring flowers...
helping to ease our fear
through years grown weary
of fighting back each tear,
seeing off the terror;
Be gaping holes, fallen towers
with time restored - only love
in hearts beating true can
build a better world

To each sacred trust broken,
bring regeneration

RUMOUR

Closed, the curtains now,
graffiti on the sill;
No cheery sounds in every room
just gloom and an eerie chill;
No laughing at the budgerigar
or thinking about a new car
but cowering in fear at a banging
on doors, the yelling
of good neighbours
out in force - after
rough justice

Empty, the garden now,
daisies on the lawn;
No kids playing on the old swing
and the satellite dish has gone;
No dog chasing next-door's cat
or neighbours at the gate
converging like wolves
on fresh meat, working up
a thirst - too late to make
a killing; the law
struck first

Media in on the act,
and prime TV;
Parents puffing their points
of view - kids enjoying
the party;
All quiet now. Werewolves
slinking from the scene;
(Can't get it right every time
and who's to say what
might have been?);
A job well done

Budgie gets to keep its cage;
History skips a page

ROUGH JUSTICE

"Guilty"

A
globular
frame

Forever
turning on
a name

Thirty pence
face at a street
party

Beggaring
belief, piling on
the agony

Higher
even than altar
brasses

Dangling
my brother
Judas

A RIVER RUNS

All's quiet on the riverbank;
All's quiet and still;
No one asks my name
or why I keep a vigil,
who cross all the time
to the other side,
moving on without a word,
heads held high
under an empty sky,
turning every now and then,
peering through a misty rain
thickening - for a glimpse
of something or someone
left behind to cling...
hear a bird sing even,
before the Dark takes all
that's ever loved and known
before this journey begun;
Eyes wide, seeking
a way through;
Hair like candles
in the wind;
Would pray, but how?
Where still waters run
but no fish swim
or rats dare make
a home

Watching the Styx river run;
Waving off the ferryman

FIRST CHRISTMAS, 2001

Empty place, empty chair…
Half-expecting a dear, familiar face
to appear at the door,
knowing Christmas will never
be the same any more, just
good times to remember
until 11th September

Life goes on, regardless
of our pain – but we shall meet again
for terrorism cannot win
and our hearts still beat as one
for all that I am lonely
in our bed and weep
till, finally, I sleep

One day, perhaps, new happiness?
For now, get through Christmas

THE LONGEST NIGHT

Through the longest night,
though angels sleeping,
a flicker of light

Brave hearts taken fright;
Sounds of weeping
through the longest night

Kind ghosts, small comfort,
their silent vigil keeping,
a flicker of light

Praying for an end in sight
of God or Man's own making
through the longest night

For one wrong come right,
some fair dawn willing,
through the longest night,
a flicker of light

DOG DAYS

Does no one see the despair on my face,
hear the anger in my heart?
Does no one understand how body and soul
are slowly coming apart?
Don't they know I'm fighting to survive,
sense a rage to live?
A curtain of mist divides body and mind,
insists on keeping us from our kind;
Stubborn, like a hound standing sentry, even
nearest and dearest refused entry;
Only the dog relates to my dumb frustrations,
dribbling on jeans you've just washed;
Fearing to bend and stroke its coat, vomit
my worst fears, stream of words;
(Noun and pronoun never came as easy to me
as 3,2,1, give a dog a bone);
No more tears, else caught at it and forced
to explain, at least try;
Needs must. For sure, a cuddle won't
muddle us through this time;
Do something. (Join forces with anger
and despair, conspiring against us?);
Mist refusing to clear, its fingers at the throat,
body and soul come apart;
Dog eyes letting hidden truths take the strain
for each just-beating heart;
I look, you look, we see. I listen. You listen.
We get talking;
Dog's tongue lolling, body and soul
start pulling together

PART FIVE

LOST AND FOUND

WHOSE FOOTPRINTS?

Footprints in the grass
might belong to anyone
enjoying a stroll
in quiet woods,
mulling over problems,
making decisions
or wishing away pain
in the rain

Footprints in the grass
pass a huge oak and pause,
listen out for Nature's
cheerful voice;
Only, no birds singing,
a grasshopper even,
just more rain clawing
at the skin

Footprints in the grass,
like old friends fallen out,
desperate to put
things right;
Suddenly, veering off
the beaten track, a spring
in each step, no
turning back

Baggy clouds starting
to break up; sun shining
through; birds singing,
a grasshopper too;
A gentler rain, letting
flowers open their hearts
like footprints
in the grass

A SPARROW FALLS

World, falling apart;
Dreary and empty, gardens
of the heart;
Senses, playing cruel
tricks - and no one
suspects;
Walking out one day,
seeing nothing - but colours
grey;
Bonding with a sparrow
in the gutter, wings a weary
flutter;
Shaking hands reach
down to hold, small comfort
grown cold;
Staring, each glassy eye;
Wrapping death gently - in
a tissue;
Suddenly, pricking up
the ears - at sounds familiar
on telegraph wires;
Sparrows, spreading time
and space, sharing their lives
with us;
Together, they depart,
dropping seeds - snatched
from the heart;
Come tomorrow's
brighter dawn, sparrows
in the garden

THE KITE

No grave to tend, but a place
to leave flowers, where last
we gathered to send you
on your way;
Fairy dust, scattered in
green fields where
once we children,
loved to play;
Fond thoughts, like the tail
of a kite dancing
in a breeze, one
long-ago day;
Let twilight come, shadows
marking time though
the Dark must have
its way;
No sign of life in fields
cut back, children
grown, lovers
gone away;
No grave to tend, but a place
to leave flowers, where last
they gathered to send us
on our way

Kite, dancing in a breeze,
trailing memories

LOST AND FOUND

Friends, family, lovers,
gone - but always part of us,
especially in twilight hours,
as we pause in quietude
to contemplate our solitude;
Each goodbye, lingering
lights in the eye over
a treasure chest

Let the exquisite amber
of a fallen leaf part exorcise
our grief. Autumn's glory
all around; winter's story
sure to keep Hope alive;
Spring flowers, heartbeats
below ground; friends,
family, lovers

Lost and found

TIME AND THE HOUR

Old friend at the door
come to borrow some sugar;
Biscuits and a cuppa,
story of our lives
together;
Over lunch and supper,
arthritis getting the better;
Trying out our wings
like born again
hatchlings;
Now and then reflecting
how things might have been;
Preferring to share
the good times
in between;
Time to go home;
Next time, my turn,
be it earth or heaven
see us fall, shoot
us down

Till then

LAST ORDERS

May the last thing I see
be a lark dropping
from the sky;
May the last thing I hear
be its sweet song
of cheer;
May the last thing I smell
be a fragrance
of flowers;
May the last dream I have
be the life that
was ours;
May the last thing I touch
be the pleasure
of your skin;
May the last thing we share
be a toast to love, in
home-made wine

Before the good earth
calls "Time"

A WAITING GAME

A young god all in white
came to me in a dream
last night;
He kissed me and held
me tight, said he missed me
and meant no harm;
In the crook of his arm,
(O, sweet seduction!)
self-destruction;
So let's start over again?
Can't beat the love
of a good man…
gone wild on a cloud,
crying aloud, gay
and proud;
Woken old and grey,
closer to you
each day

WHIPPING BOY

Should be proud
But I'm not;
Should be mad
But I'm not;
Should be glad
I'm not

Strokes of midnight

Shouldn't stay
But I do;
Shouldn't care
But I do;
Should pray
But I can't

Choices hurting

Make a run for it?
I cannot;
Throw the fight?
I will not;
Be defeated…
So what?

Curtains closing

Time, must answer
Nature's call;
At her bare feet,
Justly fall;
On my last breath,
O, Death

Use me well

SAFE AND SOUND

I hear sounds like a child crying
in my dreams, then screams...
Eyes fly open as I strain
to hear, but only wind and rain
engage my fear

A sound like someone weeping
prevents my sleeping...
Mouth flies open as I start
to work it out, but a weary sigh
kills off any shout

A hunger for the womb's bread
in my head, a lonely dread...
Soul pressing me to forgive
the bloody knot, let live
a free spirit

I hear sounds like a child crying
in my dreams, then screams...
Beside me, you stir but briefly,
arms reaching out
to save me

Snuggle close, rest, let loveless
ghosts do their worst

KISS OF LIFE

You had the smile of an angel,
white shirt flapping like wings
in a breeze;
Out of nowhere, you came,
forcing this Unbeliever
to his knees;
You took me in your arms
and kissed me, lips
on fire;
My long-smouldering body
burst into flames
of mad desire;
A passion raged in the soul
far more than purely
sexual, rose...
like the soul of a ghost
set free, into heaven
above;
It was you, named me,
shamed me into
making love;
O, ecstasy! Left for dead
and born again, to
start anew

To our hearts, be true

GUESTS AT A FUNERAL

Curtains cruelly closing,
organ surely playing;
Questions imposing doubt,
excuses running out;
Powers of reason under stress
as we ask - what happiness?
Reflecting on lost chances,
missed opportunities...
avenues unexplored, because
we were afraid...
feats of glory left for others
to make the headlines,
our own lives mostly fictions
and few surprises - like
storylines in the worst
soap operas

Never mind the tears,
enjoy the flowers

FARAWAY, SO CLOSE

In foreign fields, far away,
thousands lie in beds of clay
who gave their lives - so
humanity forever may
greet the same fair light
of dawn nor dare let
our children down
as we did them?

Under foreign skies, a weeping
for thousands left sleeping,
deserving rest, having
given of their best, all
watchmen of infernal Night
that Freedom's flame
burn yet - forever
tall and bright?

The earth is ours, its skies
delicious with sunshine
or showers, though far less
capricious than the fat cat
in our street, boasting
last year's poppy
in the lapel - of
a new coat.

Give us our daily bread;
Let live, our war dead

UNSUNG HERO

Jim was just seventeen
when war broke out;
He was courting a girl
called Jane; they held hands
at the fair, made plans for
the future, celebrated
with friends their
lives together

Jim was just eighteen
when he joined up,
all his mates did too;
Everyone admired the
uniform, waved 'em off
with royal cheers while
Jim's ma and Jane
saved their tears

Jim was just nineteen
when war took its toll,
savaged the soul till his
senses caved in and no
place to run, like a fox in
the hole, hounds hunted
down, left shivering
for sheer terror

And who'd know better
than soldiers of the crown
that a spirit once broken
is no use to anyone?
All was haste, no time
to waste, the pack denied
its reward, Jim shot
for a coward

IN GOOD COMPANY

I went to your grave on Easter day,
a longing in the heart to be near
as once we were;
I knelt, alone, unable to pray,
laid flowers at the stone,
glad to stay;
Someone wished me Peace,
said pain would pass
and hurt grow less...
that you'd left but briefly,
returned safely - to
live in me;
Only, that's not what I wanted
to hear, just be with you
as once we were;
A tugging at my sleeve
but I wept and would not,
could not leave;
Gently, lifting my face to the sky,
showing aspects of our history
like a home movie;
Easy, then, to rise and turn away
from a stone and flowers,
eternity, ours;
Walking hand in hand through
a cemetery – you and me
in good company

LOVE STORY

I sought you in summer sunshine,
among autumn leaves, in winter snow;
I found you one springtime
but had to let you go - because
the world was turning too fast,
and I lost my balance;
I'll seek again in summer rain,
weepy autumns, winter's passion
for despair, chance that Fortune cease
its creaking wheel at such a spot
where, even yet, festering wounds
might heal though worldly rot congeal;
Fool, among other names
I hear hypocrites accuse;
More to life than games
of hide-and-seek

True. Even so, no fate worse
than giving up on us

OUR SONG

When you died, a cloud
passed over the sun;
I thought I would never
smile again – but took
a long walk in pouring rain,
trying to picture your face,
listening for the timbre
of your voice;
Saw only a blur of lives
rushing past;
Heard only a sobbing, as
you took your last
curtain call;
No smiles at all - then
the sun again!
Into a rainbow, I watched
a lark soar, its cheery
song ours

Evermore

PASSAGE HOME

Having heard waves whisper
of battles lost and won
on stormy seas in faraway
places among those fighting
to keep their places - at
the wheel

Having watched clouds paint
pictures of losers, victors,
those staying on to help
dry a tear, others preferring
to turn a deaf ear - than
take the wheel

Having beached lonely shore
and coral reef, swam with
the fishes, come to grief
in oceans surreal, let heaven
take a turn - at
the wheel

Time, our seasoned captain;
Colours nailed to the mast;
Stars, moon and risen sun,
true compass at the last;
Waters of the womb,
passage home

STORAGE AND RETRIEVAL

I tied my heart with string,
used to leave it in a drawer
with two pearl buttons
and a gold hair

Like a child, I'd go there
and look, as if contemplating
the cover of a favourite
storybook

You flung open the drawer,
(par for the course, at a guess)
buried my treasure
under your shirts

Time to put away wishful
thinking, throw out buttons
and hair, let you
cut the string

You, me, like the pages
of a storybook all smudged
and yellow, left open
on a pillow

WINTER WARMERS

The hair is greyer
than yesterday;
One more furrow
on the brow;
Sight less clear, than
it used to be;
Hearing getting
worse

What now?

A loving heart beats
as yesterday;
No fewer dreams
to inspire;
Looking back, on
a good life;
Glad to chat with
old friends

By the fire

Counting blessings
in the flames;
Seeing, clearly, this
and that mistake;
Happy, just to be
who I am;
If a failure, done
my best

What the heck?

WHERE'S ROBIN?

Two people meet and fall in love,
live happy-ever-after,
though tears of grief and pain
splash sounds of joy and laughter
like drops of acid rain
in leafy evergreen

So the story goes...

Some never fall in love,
stay single ever after,
conceal tears of grief and pain
in sounds of joy and laughter,
like something obscene
in leafy evergreen

Who knows?

How love confounds!
Many the shapes, sounds
conspiring with nature
our happiness - sweet lay
of redbreast, rarely seen
in leafy evergreen

Unless we try

AS TIME GOES BY

Brown hair, shades of grey,
There's nothing I can do;
Time, slipping away

Childhood days at play,
Youth's wild ways too;
Brown hair, shades of grey

"Rejoice, rejoice!" I say
Though few dreams come true;
Time, slipping away

For every sad, blue day,
Golden moments too;
Brown hair, shades of grey

Late, love came my way
And gave my heart to you;
Time, slipping away

Together, we could not stay;
Forever, a love that's true;
Brown hair, shades of grey;
Time, slipping away

A SHORT HISTORY OF LOVE AND DEATH

We'll watch the sunset
as lovers do, wish upon a star,
wander in darkness;
Free! To kiss in open places
faces made to please;
Fingers up at regular peers,
our love as sincere as theirs
no matter the dress it wears;
O, brave new world!
Lovers everywhere
covered in stardust;
Subdued body-lust tasting wine
on Olympus;
A hymn to Dreamtime!
Cry from the heart, echo of centuries
on wings of dawn;
Sebastian cut down
by a congregation in dismay
over Judgement Day
at the Gates of Eternity

And who'll read the eulogy?

REQUIEM*

Though all my days our love I grieve,
Nor shall it be in strife,
For all you gave is all I save
And all my strength in life

In secret places once we ran,
Afraid to show we care,
Soul true but lonely, happiest only
Once our love to share

There is no death; you live in me.
This heart, though wracked with grief,
Its loss shall bear, its love to share,
Its agony but brief

The book of life, our story tells
Of desert blessed with rain,
Eternal One, each daughter, son,
Rejoice with us again

*Sung to an arrangement of The Crimmond by the London Gay Men's Chorus for *Undying Heart: a Requiem for AIDS* composed by John Harold, 1993; first included in a poetry anthology, 2002.

UNITED WE STAND

A day will come
to leave this earth
more alone than
we came to birth;
Perhaps, in pain;
Hopefully, at peace;
Ours, not to know
time or place

Nor will your face
ever lift to mine again,
to kiss, erase
tears for a lifetime
shed in ways
never quite meant;
Halcyon days
long spent

A day will come
to leave this earth
more alone than
we came to birth;
Yet we have learned
as we have grown,
fingers burned,
errors shown

A day will come,
this earthy shell break;
Love's flame…
but embers to rake;
Yet though we leave
the world alone,
let's not grieve
over a stone

Won't give Death your name;
Don't give it mine

THE QUILT MAKERS' SONG

Life! Let me not hunger
for all I cannot be, but
suffer me a passion for
what's gone before;
Let me build cathedrals,
flare them high, dedicated
to my better selves
so they may rest easy
in a shade, against crosses
made by matchstick men,
losses we shall count again
when the time comes
to account for more
than dreams. *Life, not*
all it seems

Love! Let me not beg
at the roadside, but
give freely and let's
paint pictures to last
centuries, windows
stained with all the colours
of our love-making;
Let those who come after us
be together in their turn
and lift an eye for knowing
this; and we shall share
each kiss again, again
again – we matchstick
men. *Love, not*
all our pain

Death! Let me not weep
for those I have loved;
Let there be candles lit
in each airy cathedral,
saintly with sunshine,
ringing out with rain, our
seasons come again!
Smiles of joy among the tears
to mark this, the salvation
of our fears, a passing
through chance memories,
celebration of our years;[*]
Butterfly wings across
a garden. *Dead, and
who's forgiven?*

*On a visit to San Francisco in 1999, I felt privileged to see part of this
AIDS quilt. (In some copies of *Love and Human Remains* this line is
Missing).

THE CHRISTMAS GIFT

Christmas bells ringing,
choir voices singing,
a crisp snow falling
like manna from heaven
for kids and snowmen
while I gazed from a window,
nose against the pane,
never felt so alone;
Suddenly, I saw you there,
sunshine in the hair,
so near, so far...
a dear, familiar grin
daring me rejoin
the pleasures of togetherness
and share in festivity
than bare self-pity;
Loneliness ebbing away
as, crying, I ran to play
that Christmas Day
you threw snowballs, missed
and we kissed...
red lips sweet and warm,
blue eyes forgiving
me for living;
Where snow piles your grave,
that Christmas night
we made love...
while bells rejoiced us
and angels chorused
the pleasures of togetherness
that share in festivity,
defy self-pity

BETWEEN OURSELVES

Once we talked, walked by fields
of grain, made love in a barn,
swore each other safe from harm
though Time's wicked charm let
the world grow old, turn leaves
red and gold till winter break
their hold on deciduous bough,
bury us under snow

No patch of green, just garden birds
hanging on for spring, the earth
sound asleep, a sacred promise
bound to keep though cruel winds,
acid rain - our time come again
to talk, walk by fields of grain,
make love in a barn, swear each
other safe from harm

Though country lane and fields
of grain re-shaped on demand,
raped by a highway madness that
can only end in tears, photographs
in a family album dragged out for
weddings, christenings, funerals,
no sign of a barn, only an old
garden shed

We tried

ABOUT THE POET:

R. N. Taber was born in Kent in December 1945 and graduated from the University of Kent in Canterbury, 1973. A librarian by profession, he now lives in London and works on an occasional basis in information work. Most of the poems in this volume have appeared in various poetry magazines and anthologies in the U.K. and U.S.A. during 1993 - 2002; many were written much earlier. A gay man, he writes a psychosociological poetry that views neither the gay world nor the world in general through rose tinted glasses. However, he describes himself as a positive thinker; a thread of optimism can be detected in even the most downbeat of his poems. He frequently experiments with voices. Although he often writes in the first person, many of his poems are a combination of observation, role-play and personal experience - exploring new ways of seeing and feeling.

In 1996, he published *August and Genet,* a selection of his own gay-interest poems, under the auspices of Aramby Publications - WIRE Poetry Booklets (No.12). More than three hundred poems have appeared in various U.K. and some U.S. poetry publications. His work has been placed in several national poetry competitions. Two poems have won a 2nd prize in the annual Forward Press *Top 100 Poets* competition chosen from around some 35,000 contributions to its poetry imprints during the previous year - *Ordinary People* (1999) and *A Winter's Tale* (2002). Some of his poems can also be found on select Internet sites. His first major collection - *Love And Human Remains* - has proven popular not only with readers who enjoy contemporary poetry but also among those rarely inclined towards the genre.

Your comments are always welcome. Write to Assembly Books at the address on the verso title page or e-mail RogerTab@aol.com. - "No, I don't write gay poetry, just poetry. Poetry is poetry is poetry just as people are people are people. Colour, creed, sex, sexuality...these are but parts of a whole. It is the whole that counts."

ACKNOWLEDGEMENTS:

I would like to thank all those editors and publishers who have included my work in various poetry magazines and anthologies since I first began submitting for publication in 1993. I would also like to thank friends and colleagues for their support. A special thank you to Internet friends and contacts, many of whom I have never met in person; their Instant Message comments and e-mails have provided encouragement and inspiration since I first went online in 1998 and, hopefully, will continue to do so.

Roger Noel Taber